ANCIENT MEXICAN DESIGNS

Coloring Book

MARTY NOBLE

DOVER PUBLICATIONS, INC.
Mineola, New York

Note

The magnificent artistry of ancient Mexico has survived for centuries, largely due to the preservation of surviving carvings and codexes (manuscripts). These aesthetic and iconographic works of the Aztecs, Mayas, and other Mesoamerican civilizations (encompassing all pre-Columbian peoples of southern North America), were likely used in temples or shrines as tools to divine the future or record cultural histories and rituals.

Featured in this book are highlights from two of the finest ancient Mexican codexes: the Codex Nuttall, a Mixtec work which originated in south central Mexico (the region of present-day Oaxaca) in approximately 1000 A.D., and the Codex Borgia, created by ancient Mexicans in the central or southern Puebla region, ca. 1400.

Carefully rendered from codexes, carvings, metalwork, and paintings, the designs show the range of style and technique of several ancient Mexican civilizations. The Classic period for Mesoamerican culture, as referred to in the captions, occurred between A.D. 300–900, beginning with the rise of the Teotihuacan people and ending with the decline of the Mayas.

Bibliographical Note

Ancient Mexican Designs Coloring Book is a new work, first published by Dover Publications, Inc., in 2004.

DOVER *Pictorial Archive* SERIES

This book belongs to the Dover Pictorial Archive Series. You may use the designs and illustrations for graphics and crafts applications, free and without special permission, provided that you include no more than four in the same publication or project. (For permission for additional use, please write to Permissions Department, Dover Publications, Inc., 31 East 2nd Street, Mineola, N.Y. 11501.)

However, republication or reproduction of any illustration by any other graphic service, whether it be in a book or in any other design resource, is strictly prohibited.

International Standard Book Number
ISBN-13: 978-0-486-43633-3
ISBN-10: 0-486-43633-0

Manufactured in the United States of America
Dover Publications, Inc., 31 East 2nd Street, Mineola, N.Y. 11501

Mixtec — Goldwork design

PLATE 1

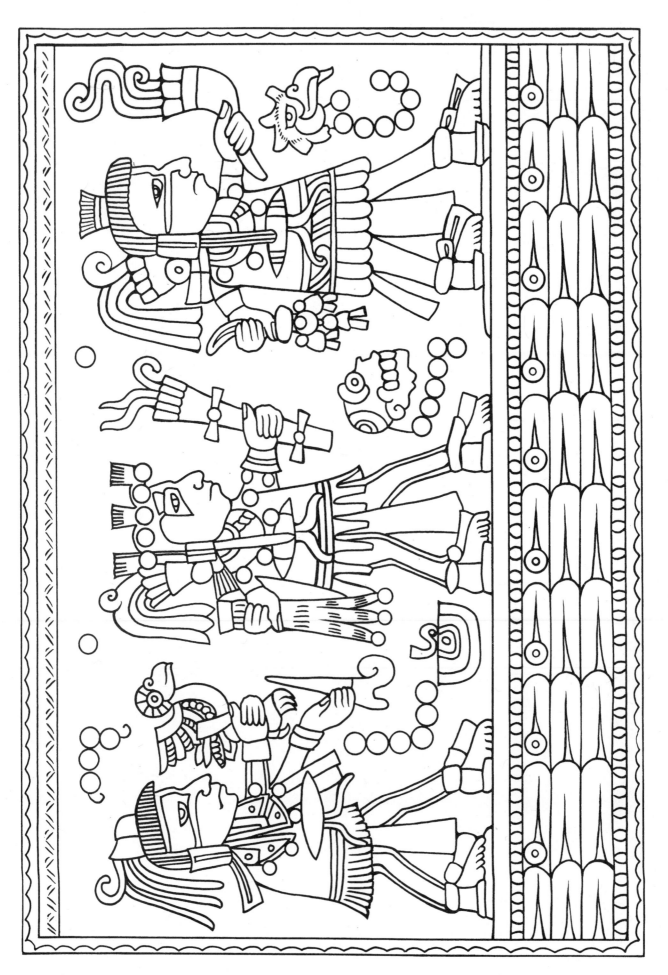

Detail from plate 18 of the Codex Nuttall.

PLATE 2

Detail from plate 19 of the Codex Nuttall.

PLATE 3

Detail from plate 20 of the Codex Nuttall.

PLATE 4

Detail from plate 21 of the Codex Nuttall.

PLATE 5

Top: Aztec — Design from the Codex Fejérváry-Mayer, depicting the Four Regions of the Universe.
Bottom: Detail from plate 23 of the Codex Nuttall.

PLATE 6

Top: Detail from plate 53 of the Codex Borgia, depicting Xochipilli ("Prince of Flowers") as a deer.
Bottom: Late-classic Maya — Bicephalic monster, Copan Altar 41.

PLATE 7

Detail from plate 21 of the Codex Borgia, depicting one of eight supernatural scenes with calendrical associations.

PLATE 8

Center: Detail from plate 35 of the Codex Borgia, depicting the initial portion of a sacred-bundle ritual performed before the Temple of Heaven. Stripe Eye, the figure on the left, may represent either a king or the god Quetzalcoatl.

Sides: Assorted figures from the Codex Borgia.

PLATE 9

Detail from plate 32 of the Codex Borgia, depicting a figure with flint-knife joints and head, out of which miniature images of Tezcatlipoca (god of darkness and war) emerge.

PLATE 10

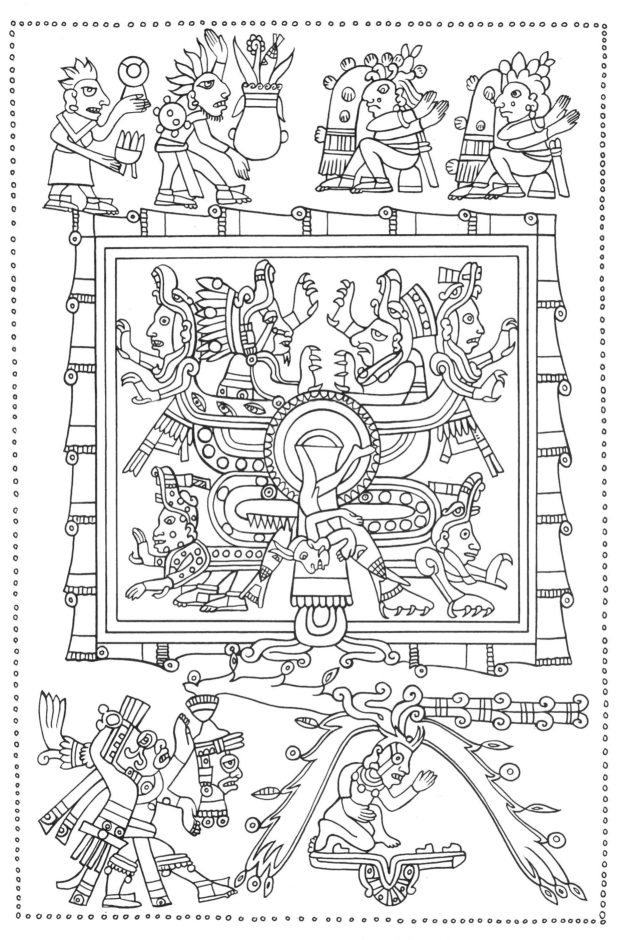

Detail from plate 38 of the Codex Borgia, depicting Stripe Eye
engaged in rituals while on a supernatural journey.

PLATE 11

Detail from plate 20 of the Codex Borgia, depicting a portion of a 260-day calendar. The figure on the right is Chalchiuhtlicue ("Jade Skirt"), goddess of running water, making a blood offering before a smoking stream that contains a fire serpent. The symbols above and below the scene represent days of the calendar.

PLATE 12

Detail from plate 72 of the Codex Borgia, depicting the four directions, each represented by a deity surrounded by a plumed serpent. Each deity carries five day signs to reflect the groupings of days delineated in other parts of the codex.

PLATE 13

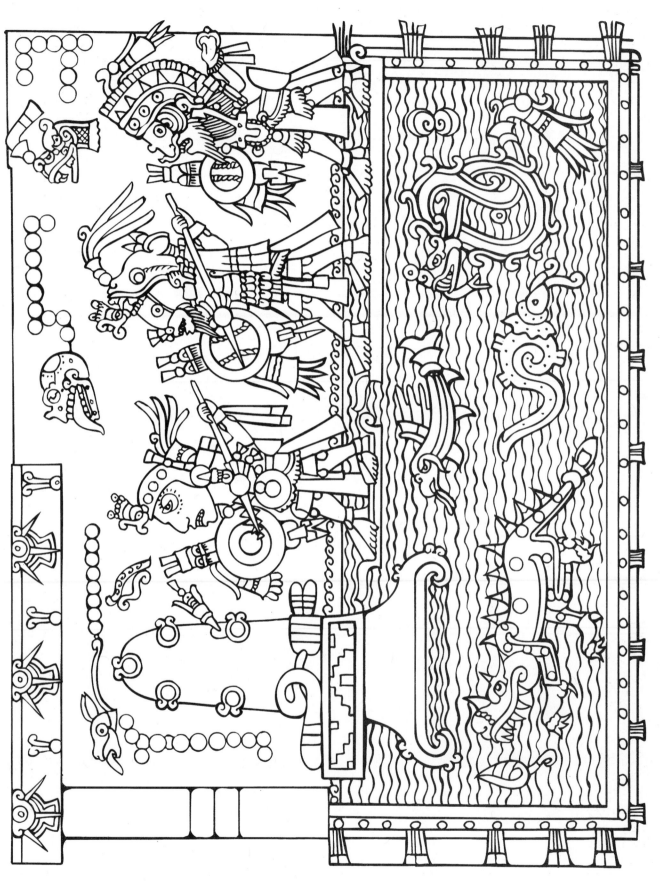

Mixtec-Zapotec — Painting from codex.

PLATE 14

Late-classic polychrome mural depicting a figure standing on a feathered serpent, Cacaxtla.

PLATE 15

Center: Birth of Tezcatlipoca from the navel of the earth deity Tlaltecuhtli.
Border: Aztec — Late post-classic design from body stamp, Tenochtitlan.

PLATE 16

Pre-Aztec — Classic-period fresco depicting a vegetation goddess, Tepantitla dwelling compound in Teotihuacan.

PLATE 17

Center: Aztec — Carving detail from a huehuetl (upright wooden drum), depicting an eagle warrior. *Border:* Flat stamp design, Jalisco.

PLATE 18

Center: Aztec — Relief design under base of the Colossal Head of the moon goddess Coyolxauhqui.
Upper Corners: Maya Toltec — Post-classic relief design from throne in the Temple of the Warriors, Chichen Itza.
Borders: Aztec — Repeated detail from aqueduct relief.

PLATE 19

Aztec — Detail from the Codex Barbonicus,
depicting Xochiquetzal ("Flower Feather"), goddess of love and flowers.

PLATE 20

Aztec — Detail from the Codex Barbonicus,
depicting Itzlacoliuhqui ("Obisidian Knife"), god of the cold.

Plate 21

Center: Aztec — Detail from the Codex Barbonicus, depicting Chalchiuhtlicue.
Top and Bottom: Mixtec-Aztec — Detail of Gilded Spear Thrower.

PLATE 22

Maya — Sarcophagus lid, depicting the great leader Pacal and religious symbols, Palenque.

PLATE 23

Center: Maya — Clay ocarina, depicting heads of gods protruding from the mouths of serpents on a priest's headdress.

Border: Maya — Column depicting a feathered serpent, used to support a temple lintel.

PLATE 24

Center: Maya — Relief design on Altar 5, Tikal.
Top and Bottom: Maya — Protoclassic design from Stela 25, depicting a caiman tree, Izapa.

PLATE 25

Left: Maya — Detail from panel of foliated cross, depicting a priest holding a jade figurine of the creation god Itzam Na, Palenque.
Right: Maya — One of two central figures on panel in Temple of the Sun, Palenque.
Bottom: Maya — Design from carved and painted stonework.

PLATE 26

Center: Maya — Stela relief design depicting a man making offerings to a deity, Piedras Negras.
Side Panels: Image of Quetzalcoatl (ancient Mexican serpent god) as feathered serpent.

PLATE 27

Maya — Detail from carved and painted wall at Jaguar Temple, Chichen Itza.

PLATE 28

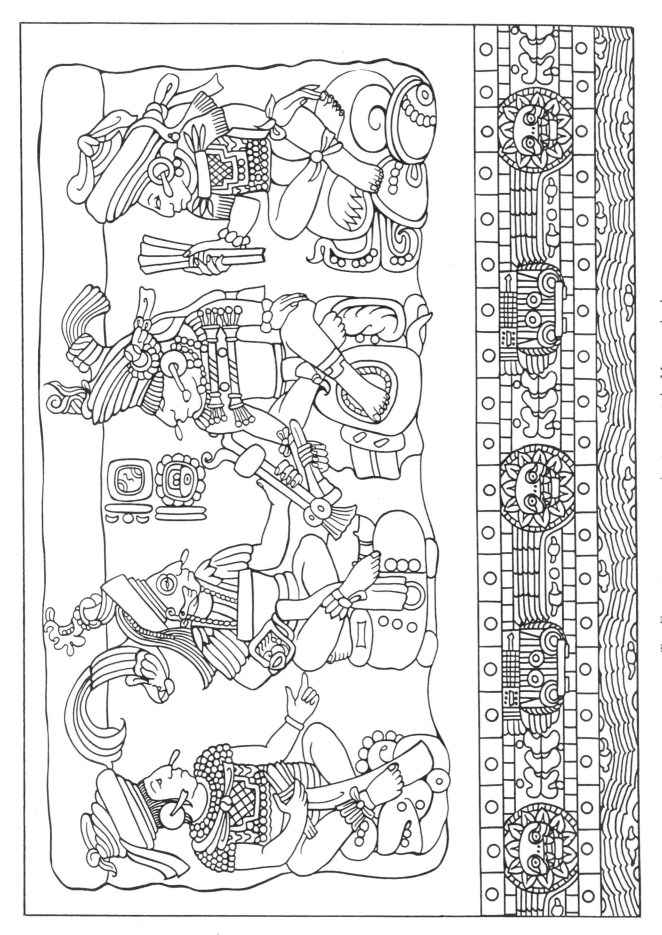

Top: Four astronomers convening to correct the Mayan calendar.
Bottom: Relief design from Altar Q at Temple of Quetzalcoatl, Copan.

PLATE 29

Maya — Relief design of Mayan king, Palenque.

PLATE 30